SMART ABOUT

MONEY a rich history

by Jon Anderson
Illustrated by Thor Wickstrom

For Larry Levy, a man of <u>very</u> rich tastes!—J.A.
To Bob, who doesn't care about money—T.W.

Cover and p. 30, courtesy of Ed Hines; p. 14, (Gaul) Werner Forman/Art Resource, N.Y., (Phonicia) courtesy of ancient-coin-forum.com, (all others) British Museum/DK Images; p. 15, (m.l., m.m.) Ancient Art and Architecture Collection, (m.r.) DK Images, (all others) British Museum/DK Images; p. 16, AP Photo/Dan Loh; p. 17, (top background) American Numismatic Association, (m.) courtesy of Fred Weinberg, (b.) Pearson Learning Group; p. 18, (state quarters) United States Mint, (m.l.) Pearson Learning Group, (m.r.) Prentice Hall School; p.19, (t., m.) American Numismatic Association, (m.,b.) Hulton Archive/Getty Images, Inc; p. 24, 29, Pearson Learning Group

Library of Congress Catalog-in-Publication Data is available.

ISBN 0-448-43205-6 (pbk)   A   B   C   D   E   F   G   H   I   J
ISBN 0-448-43284-6 (GB)   A   B   C   D   E   F   G   H   I   J

From the desk of
Ms. Brandt

Dear Class,
  We have been learning about so many exciting events from the past. Now you may choose a subject that is of special interest to you for your report.
  You may write about something that happened thousands of years ago or about something that happened not so very long ago - maybe when your parents or your grandparents were your age. It's up to you!

  Here are some questions you might want to think about:

🍎 What made you pick your topic?

🍎 Did you learn anything that really surprised you?

Good luck and have fun!
                                    Ms. Brandt

I like money. A lot! That's why I chose money as the subject of my report.

Ms. Brandt, it was fun when you had us make up our own coat of arms. In case you don't remember mine, here it is again.

my dog, Goldy

my most valuable coins

Show me the money!

I also like to make money. I make money walking dogs, mowing lawns, running errands, shoveling snow . . . you name it! I'm going to be a billionaire when I grow up. These are some of my business cards. I made them up on my computer.

RAKE-MON
"LEAF YOUR RAKING TO ME"
BILL GREEN
CHIEF RAKER-BAGGER
414-3607
372 BUCKLAND DR.

HAVE SHOVEL, WILL TRAVEL, INC.
BILL GREEN
SNOW REMOVAL SPECIALIST
372 BUCKLAND DR.
ASK ABOUT OUR CREATIVE SERVICES
414-3607

KID FOR HIRE
"NO JOB TOO SMALL"
BILL GREEN
C.E.O.
372 BUCKLAND DR.
414-3607

BILL GREEN
GRASSOLOGIST
414-3607
THE LAWN DOCTOR
"MOW FOR YOUR MONEY"

THE PUPPY MEISTER
"FOR A NEW LEASH ON LIFE"
BILL GREEN
MASTER DOG-WALKER
372 BUCKLAND DR.
414-3607

These are some of my business cards. (I made them on my computer.)

WHAT IS MONEY, ANYWAY?

I started off by looking up the word *money* in the dictionary.

mon-ey /munee/ *n.* a medium of exchange

Huh? I asked my parents what that means, and they explained it like this:

For instance, my neighbor gave me $5 for shoveling her sidewalk.

Then I spent that $5 on a bunch of *Uncle Scrooge* comic books.

Thanks to money, everyone got what they wanted. My neighbor got her sidewalk shoveled. I got my comic books. And the guy at the comic store got $5 to spend any way that he wants to. But before money existed, it wasn't that easy.

WHAT DID PEOPLE DO BEFORE THERE WAS MONEY?

Before people had money they used to do something called *bartering*. Bartering means trading one thing for another. I barter with my friend Hal all the time.

The problem with bartering is that each person has to own something that the other person wants.

That's why people invented money!

People who lived in the same area got together and picked something that they all agreed was valuable. For example, a thousand years ago in Norway, during the time of the Vikings, people decided on dried codfish. That's what they used for money!

I LOVE PAYDAY!

And 2,000 years ago, Roman soldiers were often paid in salt. Salt was hard to find in those days. It was also good for keeping meat from spoiling as well as making food taste better. The modern word *salary* comes from the Roman word for salt!

In different parts of the world, at different times in history, people used all sorts of things as money.

Corn (Guatemala)

Rice (S.E. Asia)

Dried cod (Norway)

Coconuts (Nicobar Islands)

Chocolate (Aztecs)

Almonds (India)

Salt (Rome)

Tea (Mongolia)

Barley (Babylon)

and animals (elsewhere)

There were problems with this kind of money, though.
It was often hard to carry.

And it could spoil, go bad, or be eaten.

But all over the world there was one thing people agreed
was VERY valuable—

GOLD

555 feet

Gold never went bad the way food did.
And **gold** wasn't like any other metal.
It didn't rust like iron, turn
green like copper and bronze, or
tarnish like silver. It had
many uses, for example, making fancy
jewelry, valuable cups and plates,
and other stuff like that.
Not only was **gold** beautiful,
but because there was so little
of it, people everywhere thought
it was worth a lot. Even today,
if you took all of the **gold** that's
ever been found and made it into
bricks, you would only have
enough to build a solid block as
tall as the first fifty-five feet of the
Washington Monument!

55 feet

me

It would take all the gold in the world just to build this much of the Washington Monument!

FUN GOLD FACTS!

After they died, Egyptian pharaohs (such as King Tut) were buried with lots of **gold** so they'd still be rich in the next world.

weee!

The Aztecs, who lived in what is now Mexico, made beautiful objects out of **gold** and then threw them into deep wells as gifts to their gods.

GLITTER ST.

Myth?

Yeth.

When explorers first came to the American Southwest, they were looking for the Seven Cities of Cibola, which supposedly had so much **gold** that the streets were paved with it. Nobody ever found the cities.

The largest **gold** nugget ever was found in Australia in 1869. It weighed 154 pounds, and today would be worth at least a million dollars.

Me
89
Pounds

Nugget
154
Pounds

FORT KNOX

The most **gold** in the world today belongs to the U.S. government and is kept in Fort Knox in Kentucky. No one gets in to see it, though.

It was also easy to make **gold** into big pieces that were worth a lot and smaller pieces that weren't worth as much. From there, it was just a short jump to the greatest invention in the history of money . . .

COINS!

Coins were invented more than 2,500 years ago in the kingdom of Lydia. That's where the country of Turkey is today. The coins were made from a mixture of gold and silver.

Lydian coin

Norway

Saxony (England)

Denmark

Belgium

Oldbia (Russia)

EUROPE

Gaul (France)

Greece

Lydia (Turkey)

Carthage (Spain)

Rome

Babylon (Iráq)

Carthage (Tunisia)

Phoenicia (Lebanon)

Morocco

Egypt

AFRICA

Tanzania

Different sized coins had different values, so it was now possible to set an exact value on an item, as well as make change. Plus, the coins were easy to carry. Everyone liked the idea so much that it quickly spread everywhere!

ASIA

Japan →

Holes for
threading
coins on
strings

China →

Pakistan ↓

ia →

India ↓

Thailand ↓

HOW COINS ARE MADE!

The process of making coins is called *minting*, and the place where coins are made is called a mint. Don't confuse it with the mints that make your breath smell better.

Mint

mints

The U.S. Mint in Philadelphia

Last summer we visited the largest mint in the world. It's in Philadelphia. Along with another mint in Denver, it makes all the coins that are used in the United States. When the coins are brand-new and in perfect shape they're said to be in *mint condition*. Now the term is used for practically anything that's in perfect shape (like comic books or trading cards), whether it was made in a mint or not.

Up until 1965, coins were made of silver (dollars, half dollars, quarters, and dimes), or nickel (nickels, of course!), or copper (pennies). But today they're all made from a metal that's a mix of copper and nickel and is called cupronickel.

RECIPE CARD

MAKE YOUR OWN CUPRONICKEL

INGREDIENTS:
• COPPER BARS
• NICKEL PELLETS

Melt all the ingredients and mix together well. Pour onto ingot mold and let cool.

YIELD: MANY INGOTS OF CUPRONICKEL

To make coins, they take bars (called *ingots*) of the cupronickel and press them into smooth, flat sheets. A steel press punches out a circle called a blank, and then another machine gives the blank a raised rim. Finally, another machine stamps a picture on each side of the blank.

flat sheet of cupronickel

blanks

rimmed blanks

All U.S. coins have the same two phrases stamped on them: In God We Trust and *E Pluribus Unum* (that's Latin for "out of many, one"– like our fifty states which make up one country).

finished coins

Collecting Coins

I love collecting coins because there are so many different kinds. If you find certain coins, they can be really valuable, but mostly it's just fun to collect them. Right now I'm collecting quarters of each of the fifty states. I'm trying to find two of each state; one with a "D" on the front to show it was minted in Denver, and another with a "P" for Philadelphia.

D   P

Here are the coins for the original 13 colonies!

A person who collects coins is a called a numismatist. Try saying that five times fast!

If a coin is scarce (meaning that there aren't very many of them), it can become especially valuable.

Here are a couple that I wouldn't mind having in my collection!

In 1943, during World War II, copper was needed for weapons and equipment in the war, so pennies were made from zinc and steel instead. These pennies are the only U.S. coins that will stick to a magnet! When they started making the special 1943 pennies, though, there was still some copper left in the coin-making machine, so the first forty or so coins to come out were copper. If you were to find a 1943 copper penny today, it would be worth more than $80,000!

The last regular U.S. coin made out of gold was the 1933 Liberty double eagle $20 coin. It was called the "*double eagle*" because back then, the $10 gold coin was called an *eagle*. Only one of these 1933 double eagles still exists, and it recently sold for $7,600,000!

PAPER MONEY

Because China didn't have a lot of valuable metals, people tried using coins made out of iron, but they were really heavy! So about a thousand years ago, they started depositing (that means keeping) the heavy, iron coins at banks. The banks gave people paper receipt slips for when they wanted to get their coins back. After a while, people began to use the slips of paper as money. That's how paper money started!

← Here is what some ancient Chinese money looked like.

A man named Marco Polo, who was from Venice, went to China in 1295. When he came home he told people about paper money. But no one liked the idea. It was almost 400 years before Sweden, in 1661, became the first country in Europe to start using paper money!

In order to get people to use paper money, in the United States, the government had to promise that it could be traded in for an equal amount of gold or silver at any time.

This old $20 bill could be traded for $20 of gold.

This old $5 bill could be traded for $5 of silver.

After people finally got used to the paper money, the government stopped letting people trade it in for silver or gold. Today, people just accept that the paper money printed by the U.S. government is valuable.

During the Civil War, the South, which called itself the Confederate States of America, issued its own money. After the South lost the war, these Confederate dollars weren't worth anything, because there wasn't a government to back them up anymore.

Paper money is printed in Washington, D.C. at the Bureau of Engraving and Printing (which is also part of the U. S. Mint).

Here's a map of Washington, D.C.
The arrow shows where they print the money.

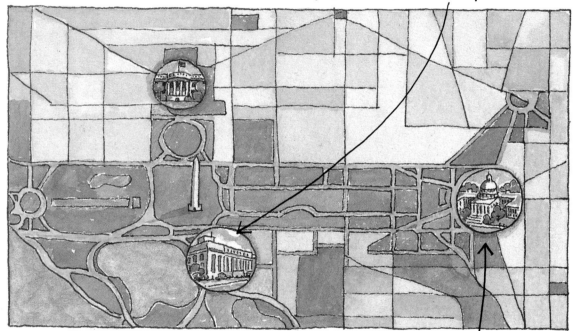

I lined up with my family really early one morning for the free passes they give out to take a tour. On an average day, almost $700,000,000 gets printed!

(my dad says that this is where they spend it.)

ER MONEY

Money is printed on large sheets of special paper. On each sheet there are thirty-two bills. Because paper money wears out so fast, the government has to print lots of money to replace the worn-out bills.

If you got your hands on all of the money that's out there you would have:

$539,890,223,079

The tour guide told us this, but later, I looked it up on the Bureau's website to see if the amount had changed at all. You can check, too, at: www.bep.treas.gov.

Sheets of money go through three printing steps. First, the back side gets printed with green ink. Then the front side gets printed with black ink. Finally, the front is printed again with a special seal and a set of numbers that make each bill different from all others. The money is then given out by special government banks called the Federal Reserve. There are twelve of these banks in different parts of the country.

The letter on a $1 bill tells you which one of the twelve Federal Reserve banks released it.

A	is from	Boston
B		New York
C		Philadelphia
D		Cleveland
E		Richmond
F		Atlanta
G		Chicago
H		St. Louis
I		Minneapolis
J		Kansas City
K		Dallas
L		San Francisco

If you live in San Francisco and have a bill with an "B" on it, you know that bill has traveled all the way from New York!

When I was on the tour, I also asked about the weird pyramid with the eye above it that's on the back of a dollar bill. I learned that the pyramid represents the United States (the Roman numerals on the base say 1776), and that it's unfinished because there is always something more that we can do to make our country better. The eye means that God is watching over us.

yucky pollution

Paper money wears out fast! The average dollar bill only lasts 22 months. When worn-out money comes back to the Treasury, it gets destroyed. They used to burn old money, but that caused too much pollution. Now it's shredded!

ACME
MONEY
SHREDDER

ACME
MONEY
HAULERS

clean shredded money

ACME
WE DO EVERYTHING
MONEY BURNING
FACTORY

Good thing I'm honest!

ACME
MONEY
HAULERS

It's still sad.

HOW TO MAKE GEORGE WASHINGTON STAND ON HIS HEAD!

Here's a fun trick I learned.
Step 1: Take a $1 bill and hold it facing you, right side up.
Step 2: Folding it the long way, fold the top half over the bottom half.

Step 3: Fold the left half behind the right half.

Step 4: Unfold the front portion to the left.

Step 5: Unfold fully. George is on his head!

PHONY MONEY!

As long as there has been money, there have been people who have tried to make fake money. It's called *counterfeiting*, and it's against the law. In the United States, the punishment for counterfeiting money is fifteen years in jail!

During the Civil War, the government figured out that as much as *half* the money being used in the country was fake! So the Treasury Department created the Secret Service to catch counterfeiters! Today, they have another job, too—protecting the President of the United States!

threads

The paper that money is printed on is very special. In fact it's against the law for anyone to make paper that is anything like money paper! It's made of 75% cotton and 25% linen, and it has teeny, tiny red and blue threads in it. If you look really closely, you see them.

This is to help make it difficult for anyone to make phony money. But there are other things you can look for to see if your money is real.

There are all sorts of other really cool things to look for on money that show whether it's real or not. Take a look at a $10 bill.

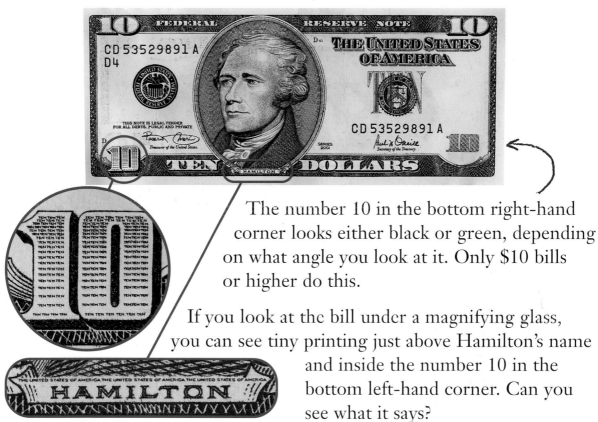

The number 10 in the bottom right-hand corner looks either black or green, depending on what angle you look at it. Only $10 bills or higher do this.

If you look at the bill under a magnifying glass, you can see tiny printing just above Hamilton's name and inside the number 10 in the bottom left-hand corner. Can you see what it says?

The words *United States of America* appear above Hamilton's name, and the word *ten* is repeated over and over inside the number 10.

If you hold the bill up to a strong light, you can see a thin strip called a *security thread* to the right of Alexander Hamilton. If you hold the bill under ultraviolet light, the strip shows up orange!

Under a strong light, you can see a faint blotch called a *watermark* on the far right side that looks like another picture of Alexander Hamilton.

WHO DECIDES WHO

The U. S. Mint is part of the Treasury Department. The person in charge is the Secretary of the Treasury. The Secretary gets to decide whose picture goes on our money.

Abraham Lincoln's face was put on the penny in 1909 to celebrate the 100th anniversary of his birth. It was the first time that a real person was pictured on U.S. money.

I thought that I would look great on a new $500 bill.

But then I found out that only dead people can be pictured on money.

GOES ON MONEY?

Right now, only eleven people have their picture on U.S. money:

MONEY OF THE FUTURE

In the future, people probably won't use coins or paper money at all. In fact, most of the money being used today is actually electronic! The money that my mom makes at her job is transferred electronically from her company's bank account to her bank account. She then pays bills using a computer to transfer money from her account...all with no paper money ever exchanging hands!

People also use plastic money. Of course, you know it better as credit cards, but it just goes to show that money can exist in lots of different forms.

And even if I can't get my picture on paper money, someday I can have my picture on a credit card, which is sort of like having my face on money after all!

Dear Bill,
Reading your report was fun. Have you read *Money* by Joe Cribb in the Eyewitness series? I know you would like it.
Ms. Brandt